Climbing on the Edge

STACKPOLE
BOOKS

0 11557 02804 1

FOTO DI SILVIO CAPAUL

WE SUPPORT TIBETAN PEOPLE

Welcome again to our appointment with "Millennium". This is the third time we meet: the first was with "Millennium"; the second with "Millennium 2000" and now we get together again with "Millennium Experimenta".

The first two issues were based on a classical, historical and a somewhat establishment view of the mountain environment. With this third one we are trying to gain momentum and to explore new territories. We didn't feel it was necessary to explain to our friends, the photographers, what we meant by

E D I T O R I A L

"Experimenta", we wanted them to feel free to offer their own interpretations.....their individual forms of self expression through photography.

The result is an "Experimenta" by computer, Experimenta and the redefinition of the boundaries of climbing, Experimenta with new, unusual and funny situations. Each picture has been chosen as we feel it embodies the concept of "Experimenta". We have managed to maintain the twelve sections (even though it was the hardest part of our work) though we still consider the mountain as a single entity constructed from many different components. Again, we would like to thank all our friends, the old ones and the new, who have contributed to this project. Thank you for sending us your best pictures, thank you for being with us and finally thank you for helping us to maintain this world wide vision of our mountains. As always we hope to meet you again on these pages and wish you moments of joy, not just admiring these images but also throughout the whole of the coming year.   **Betta and Gioachino**

We would like to continue
this dialogue with the mountains
through your images,
so if anybody
is interested please get in touch.

Grivelart - Betta Gobbi - P.O. Box 76
- 11013 Courmayeur (AO) - Italy.
Phone: 0039.0165.843714
Fax: 0039.0165.844800
Email: grivelart@grivel.com

C O N T E N T S

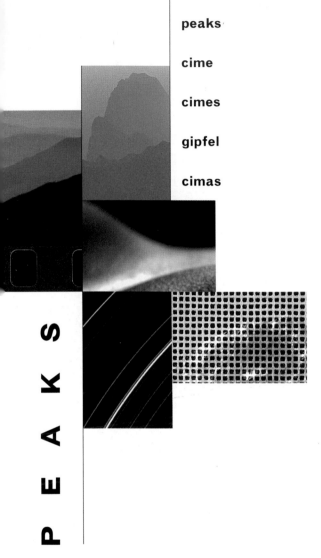

peaks

cime

cimes

gipfel

cimas

P E A K S

Cerro Torre
Patagonia,
Argentina,
Ph. Jakob Helbig.

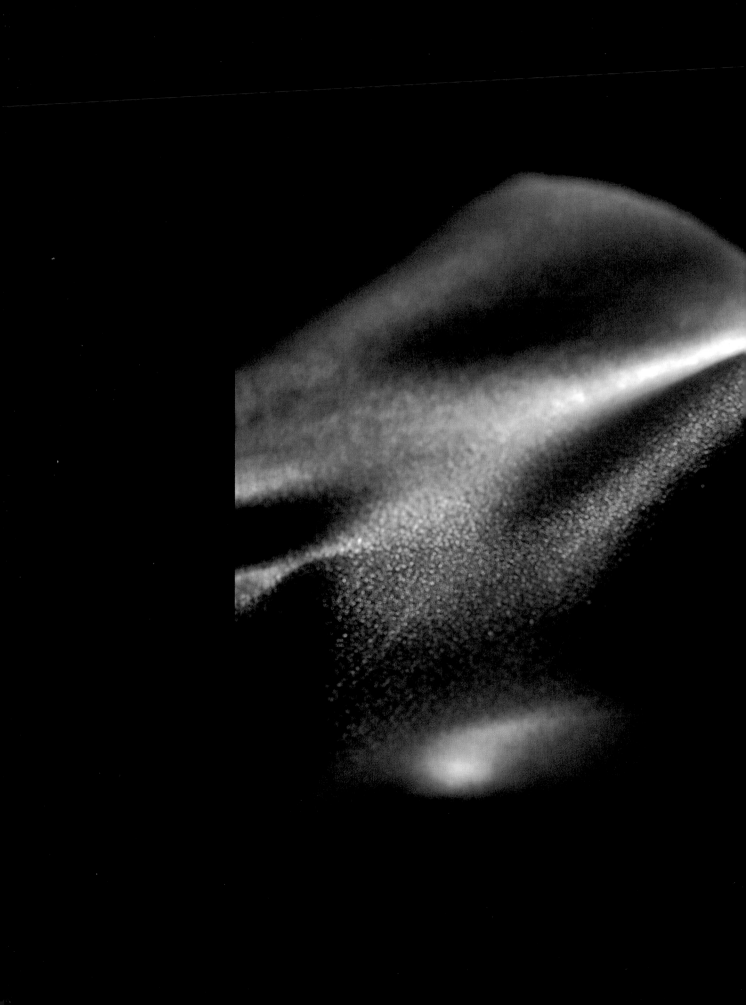

Sun rising
Alpes Maritimes
France,
Ph. Philippe Rebreyend.

where i roamed the wilderness day after day after day,
unexpected mountains appeared on my computers...

Blue Moon Mesa

Gérard Kosicki

A landscape of the imagination

sand and stone corridors
forgotten geography
outcroppings
holy places

twin formations
silence and solitude
a territory that has meaning and the power
to teach and protect

where nothing is as it appears

looking from here
teased by subtle hues of blue

+ 1

interrupted space

Mesa

Mont Blanc Italy,
Virtual Interpretation,
Ph. Flavio Faganello.

**Black Horn - Dolomites,
Italy,
Virtual Interpretation,
*Ph. Flavio Faganello.***

Mont Blanc
Italy,
Ph. Eleonora Greco.

Mt. Zervoi
Belluna Valley
Italy,
*Ph. Giandomenico
Vincenzi.*

K2 from Broad Peak
Karakorum,
Pakistan,
Ph. Robert Bösch.

Peaks,
Ph. Xavier Murillo.

Cirque de L'Homme
Oisans, France,
Ph. Sebastien Constant.

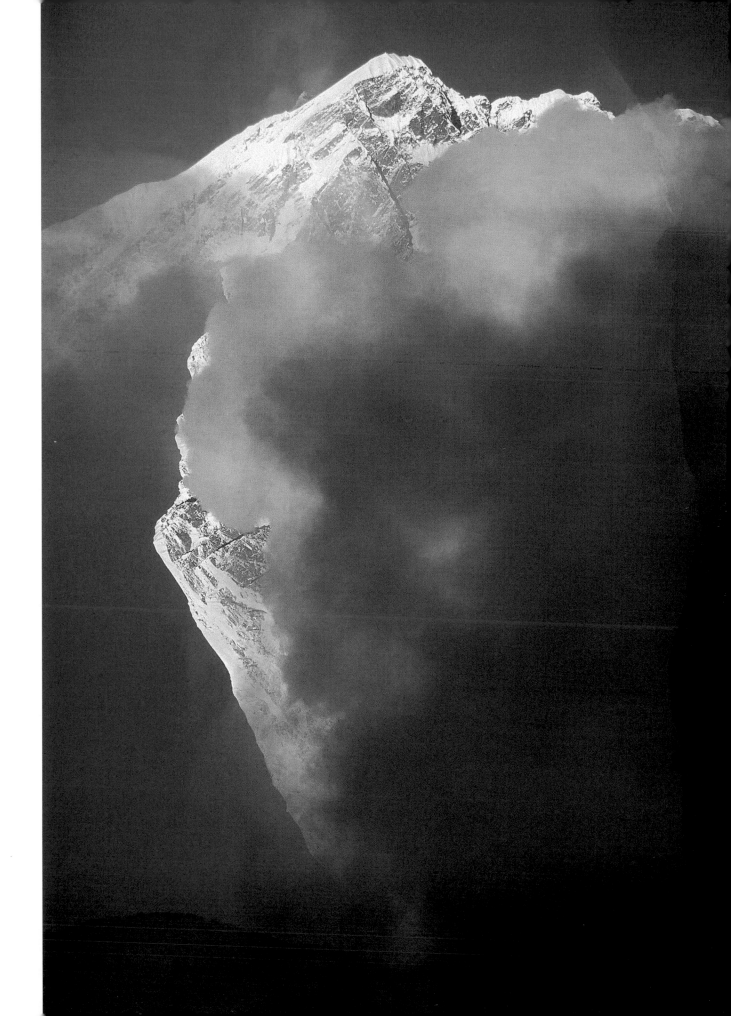

Earth Water Wind Fire

Terra Acqua Vento Fuoco

Terre Eau Vent Feu

Erde Wasser Wind Feuer

Tierra Agua Viento Fuego

EARTH WATER

WIND FIRE

Sunny rain
Jail House Cliff,
California,
USA,
Ph. Guillaume Vallot.

Alaska,
Ph. Peter Mathis.

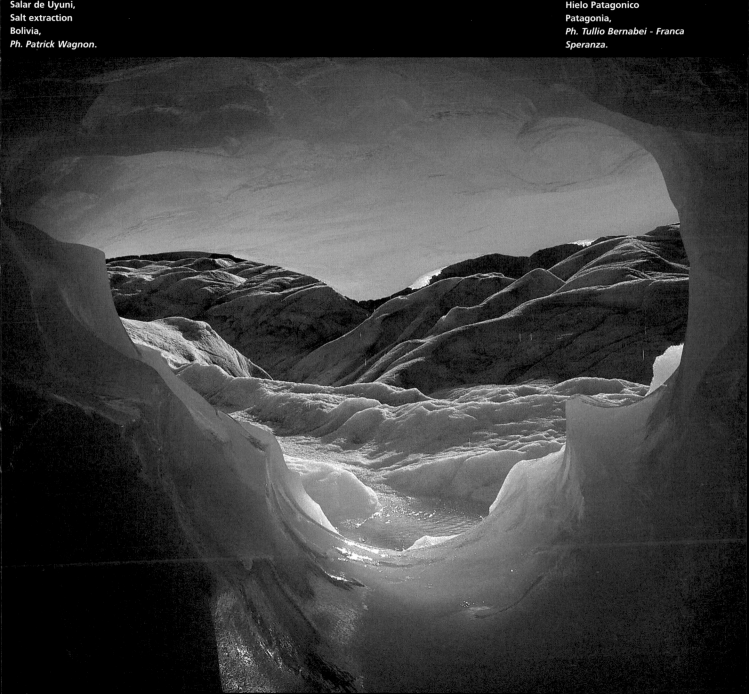

Salar de Uyuni,
Salt extraction
Bolivia,
Ph. Patrick Wagnon.

Hielo Patagonico
Patagonia,
Ph. Tullio Bernabei - Franca Speranza.

Ice wall
Antarctica,
Queen Maud Land,
Ph. Anders Modig.

Rivière Malbaie
Quebec, Canada,
Ph. Manu Ibarra

Karimsky Volcano
Kamtchatka, Russia,
*Ph. Mark Buscail -
Rapsodia.*

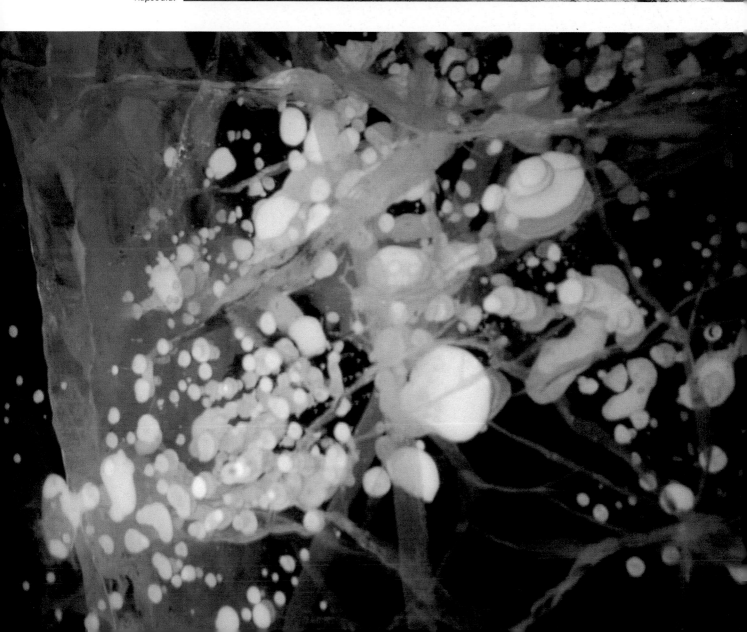

Theodore Roosevelt
National Park USA,
Ph. Tuan Luong -
Rapsodia.

"Rocksock"
Bourg St. Maurice,
France,
Ph. Wilfried Zwaans.

South Lipez
Bolivia,
Ph. Laurent Bouvet -
Rapsodia.

Basalt formations
Vik, Iceland,
Ph. Eduardo Velasco.

Ph. Stéphanie Têtu -
Sylvain Dumaine.

Seracs -
Argentière Glacier,
France,
Ph. Pierre-Alain Treyvaud.

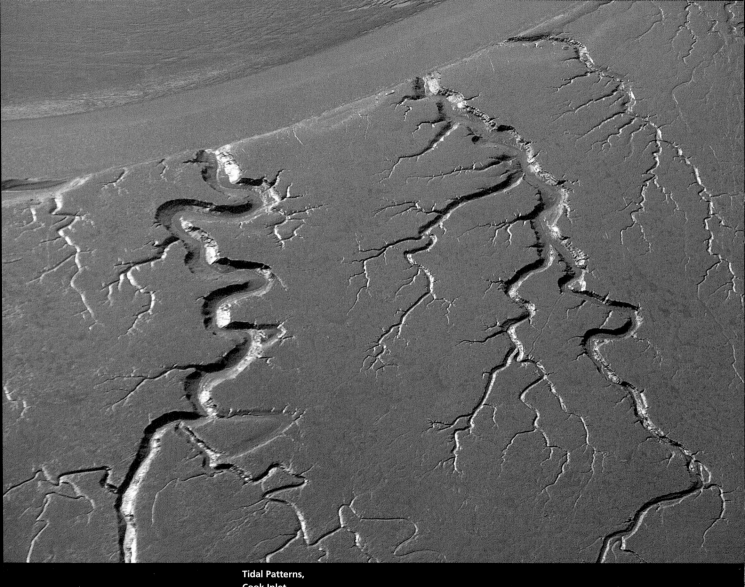

Tidal Patterns,
Cook Inlet.
Alaska,
Ph. Kennan Harvey.

Colorado River
USA,
Ph. Peter Mathis.

"The Dove"
Etna, Italy,
Ph. Patrick Gabarrou.

Fire
Hohenems, Austria,
Ph. Peter Mathis.

Wadi Rum
Jordan,
Ph. Robert Bösch.

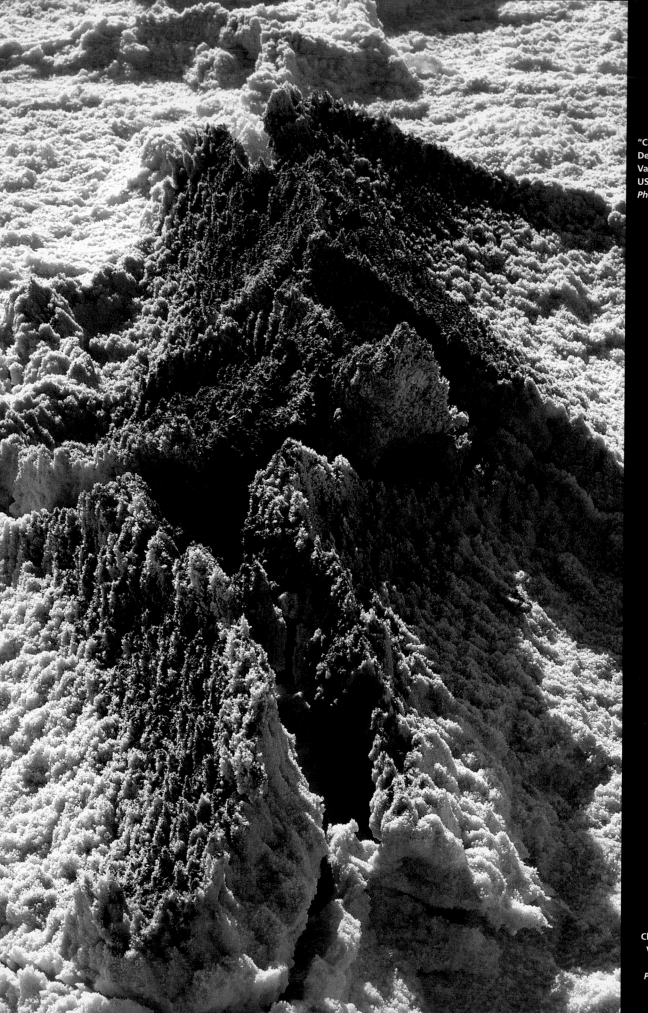

"Crystal Eruption",
Devil' Golf Course, Deat
Valley,
USA,
Ph. Andi Hechenberger.

Che Guevara "on ice"
Valloire, Maurienne,
France,
Ph. Gian Luca Boetti.

Rainstorm,
St. Rhémy-en-Bosses
Aosta Valley,
Italy,
Ph. Paolo Meitre Libertini.

Zambezi river
Africa,
Ph. Sylvie Chappaz.

Fauna Flora

Fauna Flora

Faune Flore

Fauna Flora

Fauna Flora

FAUNA

FLORA

Frozen needles
Varrone Valley,
Italy,
Ph. Federico Raiser.

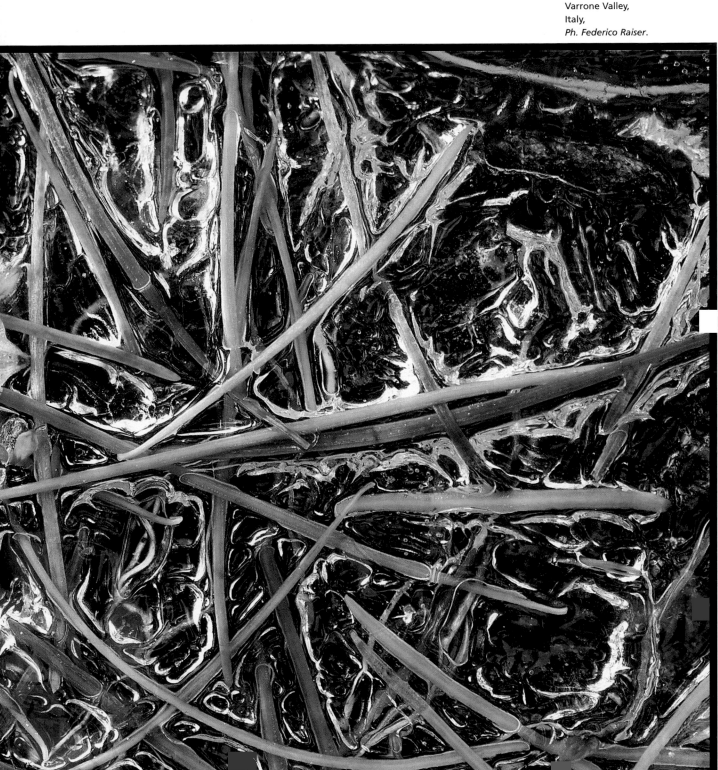

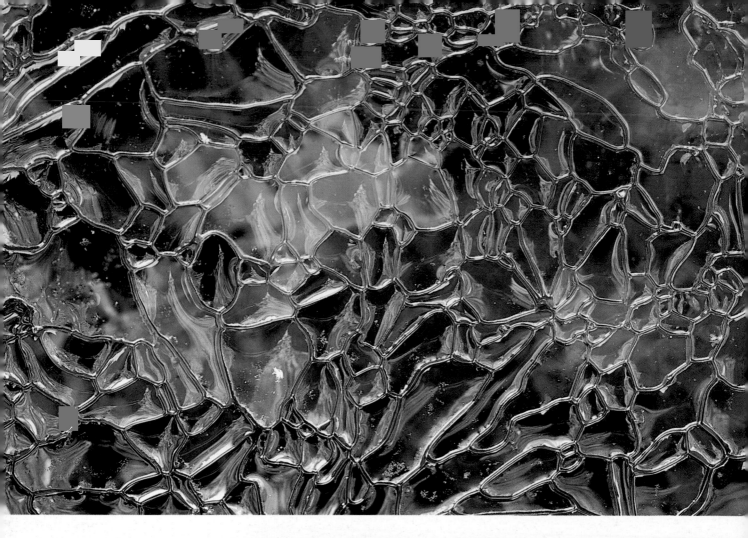

Frozen leaves
Ratti Valley
Lombardia, Italy,
Ph. Federico Raiser.

Frozen blueberry leaves
Lyngen Alps, Norway,
Ph. Pierre-Alain Treyvaud.

Mountain iris
Spain,
Ph. David Munilla.

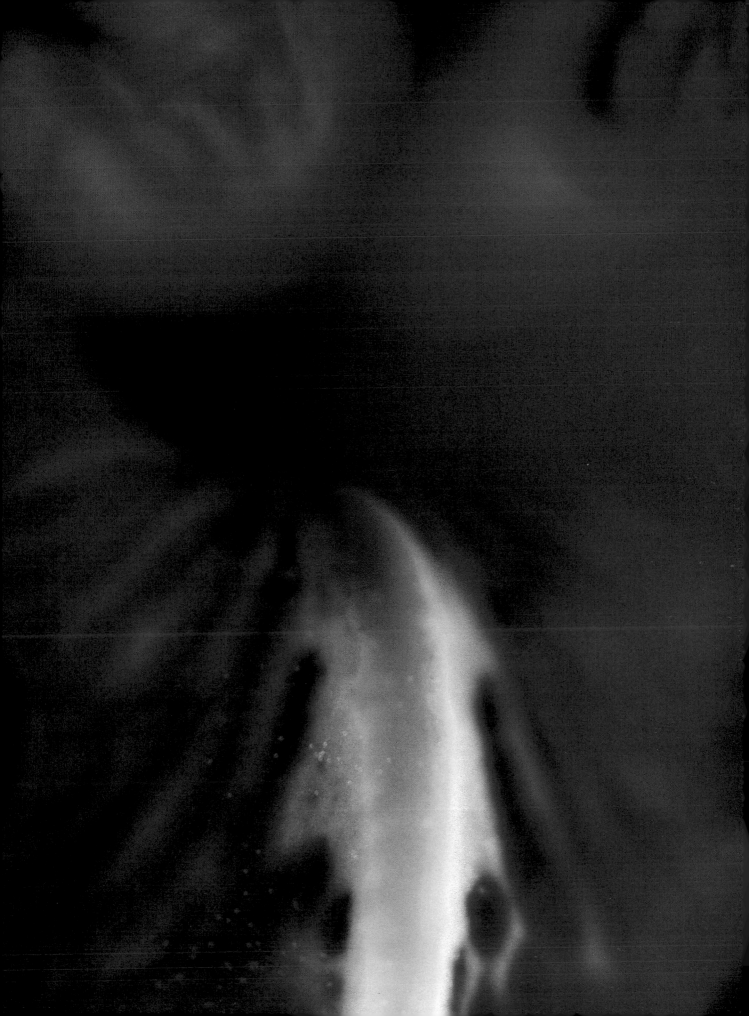

Wrinkles:
Poppy and hands
Italy,
Ph. Mario Verin.

Bald eagles
in snowstorm
Alaska, USA,
Ph. T.Mangelsen
Franca Speranza

Arctic fox in a blizzard
Manitoba
Canada,
Ph. Galen Rowell -
Franca Speranza.

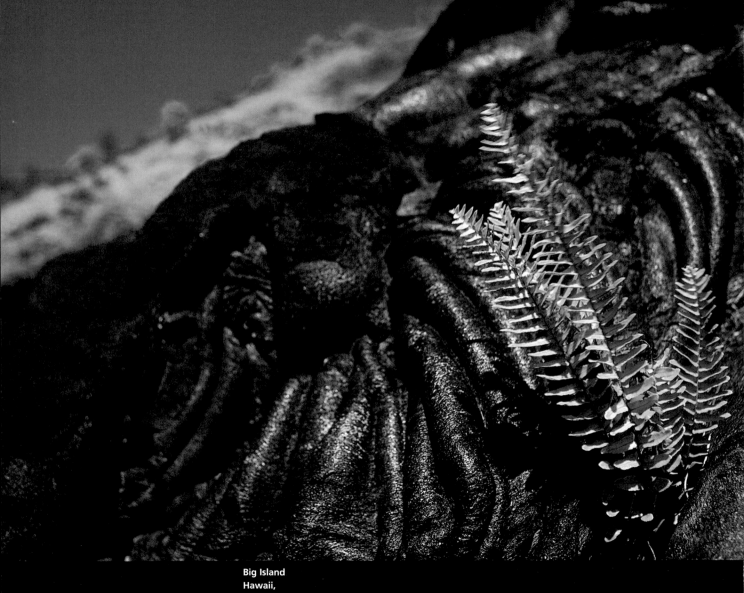

Big Island
Hawaii,
Ph. Philippe Rebreyend.

Baobab bark
Ruaha National Park,
Tanzania,
Ph. Mario Verin.

Forest,
Sweden,
Ph. Christian Aslund.

Bristlecone pine
King Canyon -
National Park,
USA,
*Ph. Tuan Luong -
Rapsodia.*

Antarctic Skua
Husvik,
South Georgia
Antarctica,
Ph. Anders Modig.

Memories of cows
Germany,
Ph. Klaus Fengler.

Rock Climbing

Sulla Roccia

Grimper

Klettern

Escalada en Roca

ROCK CLIMBING

Gudrun Innreiter
Indoor Bouldering
Austria,
Ph. Andi Hechenberger.

Steve McClure
Profit of Doom E5/6b
Curbar,
Great Britain,
Ph. Wilfried Zwaans.

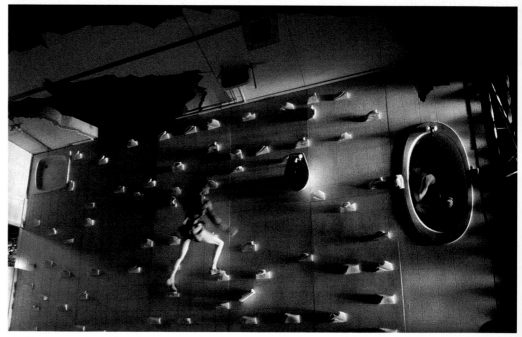

Climbing ballet
Rock and Lichen Company
Avignon festival
France,
Ph. Manu Ibarra.

François Lombard
on Belté Geuze 7c
Le Fournel
France,
Ph. Wilfried Zwaans.

FORCIBLE BALANCING ALONG DARK
LINES IN SEARCH FOR AMPLENESS/
AMPLENESS WHICH REDUCES TO
COMPLETELY YOURSELVES/ FINDING
CALMNESS IN YOURSELF
BALANCING FROM
OPPRESSIVE
PLACES
AWAY

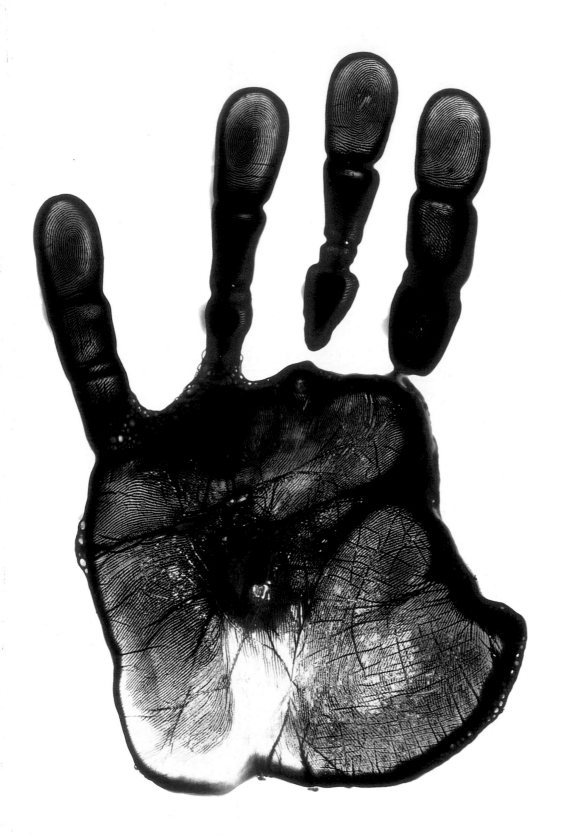

"It's a sweaty
hand-print,
oh my God!",
Ph. Wilfried Zwaans.

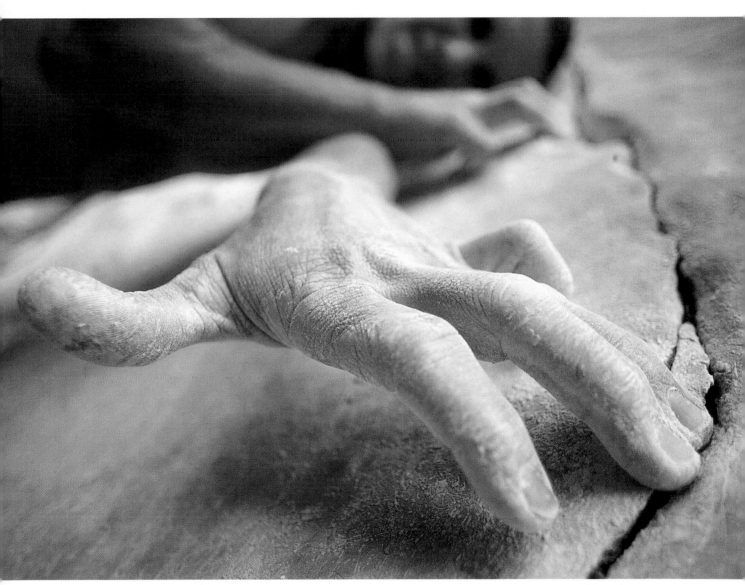

Bouldering hand
Justin Bastien
California, USA,
Ph. Corey Rich.

Daniel Du Lac training
at U.F.R.A.P.S. laboratory
Grenoble, France,
Ph. Roberto Fioravanti.

Free Climbing
World Championship
Stéphanie Bodet
Chamonix, France,
Ph. Roberto Fioravanti.

Peter Keller
bouldering Chironeco
Switzerland,
Ph. Rainer Eder.

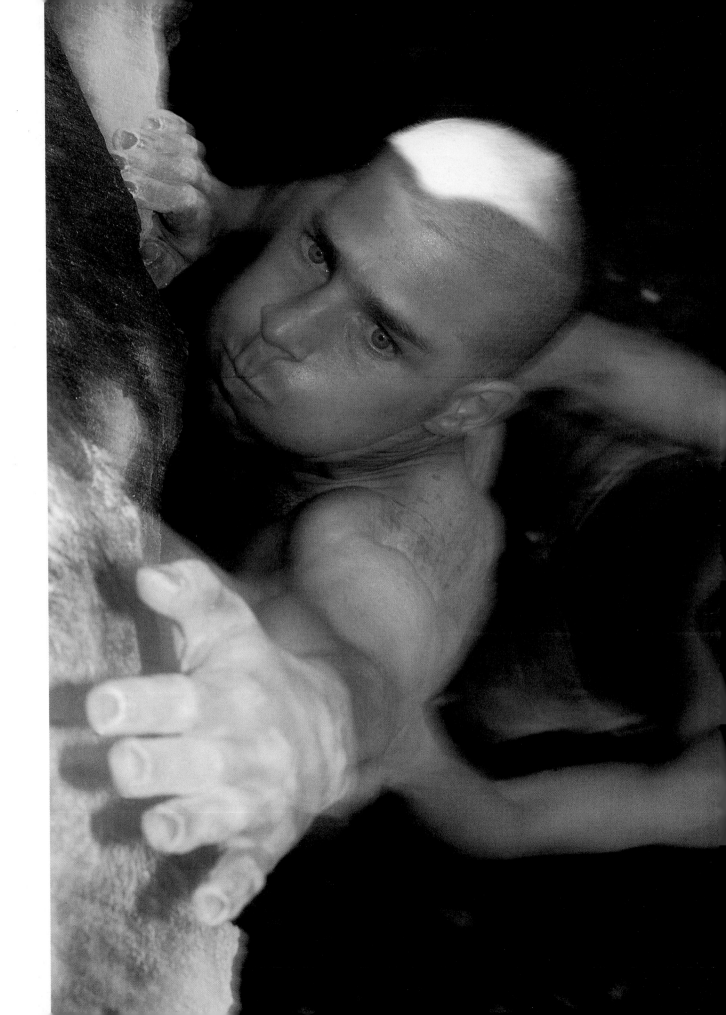

"François Lombard"
inspiration for
Maksym Petrenko
Serre Chevalier
Intl. climbing contest,
France,
Ph. Guillaume Vallot.

Justin Bastien
"Buildering"
Salt Lake City,
UTAh, USA,
Ph. Corey Rich.

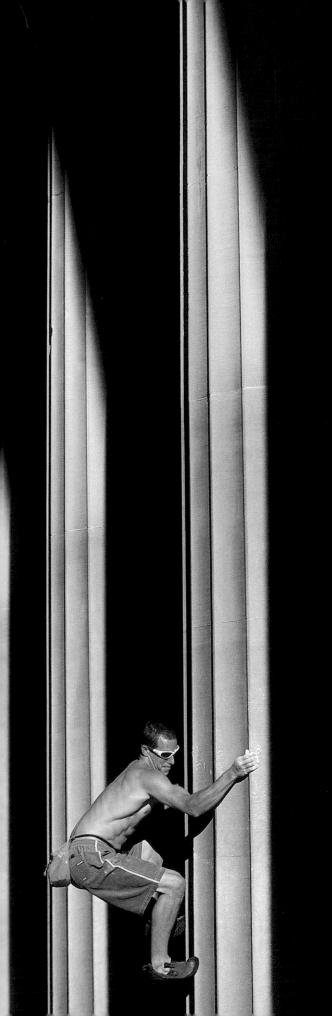

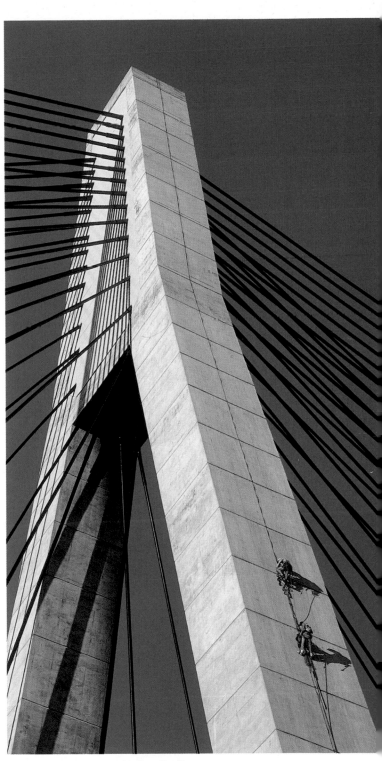

Mathew Swaite
and Owen Prall
Illegal ascent
Sydney's Glebe
Island Bridge, Australia,
Ph. Simon Carter.

Cristian Lupiòn
"Tres Techos" 8b+
El Chorro,
Màlaga Spain,
Ph. David Munilla.

Stefan Glowacz
practicing
Grotta di Biddiriscottai,
Cala Gonone,
Sardinia, Italy,
Ph. Klaus Fengler.

Pierre Guilbaud
Tours St. Jacques
Alèves, France,
Ph. Laurent Bouvet -
Rapsodia.

Fork lightning
Monstruo
de las Galletas, 8a+
Hoz del Jùcar, Cuenca,
Spain,
Ph. David Munilla.

**Céline Marceau
Isalo window
Madagascar,
*Ph. Laurent Bouvet -
Rapsodia.***

**Carlos Ruiz bouldering
in a snow storm
Pedriza,
Madrid Spain,
*Ph. David Munilla.***

Stevie Haston
Elephant Trunk
Gozo, Malta,
*Ph. Laurence
Gouault.*

Cristian Brenna,
Marzio Nardi
Mt. Brojon, Italy,
Ph. Andrea Gallo.

Marie Guillet
Mont Dauphin
France,
Ph. Wilfried Zwaans.

**Stefan Siegrist
Emosson dam
Switzerland,**

**Lynn Hill on sighting
Archimedes
Principle, 5.12b**

ICE CLIMBING

Ice Climbing

Sul Ghiaccio

Glace

Eisklettern

Escalada en Hielo

"Bubu" Mauro Bole
Reptile M10,
first ascent on sight Vail,
Colorado, USA,
Ph. Andrea Gallo.

"The Gladiators
of ice-climbing",
Ph. Marco Troussier.

J.C. Lafaille
Fatman and Robin, Vail,
Colorado, USA,
Ph. Philippe Poulet.

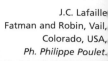

Jean-Philippe Villemaire
Courchevel

Dimitri Bitchkov
Dry-tooling
Ore, Ice World Cup 2000
Sweden,
Ph. Guillaume Vallot.

"Bubu" Mauro Bole
Cortina,
Ice World Cup 2000,
Italy,
Ph. Max Berger.

Will Gadd
Toni Lamiche
Cortina, ice world cup 2000
Italy
Ph. Philippe Pellet.

Kirov, Ice World Cup 2000
Russia,
Ph. Max Berger.

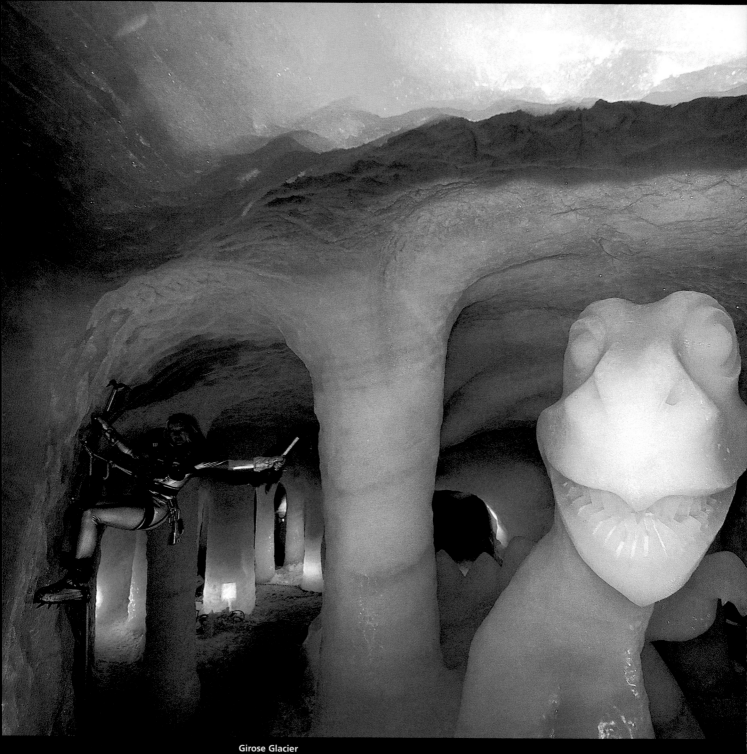

Girose Glacier

Ice Angel
Professor Falls, Alberta
Canada,
Ph. Brad Wrobleski.

Stevie Haston
The empire strikes back
M11, First Ascent
Valgrisenche, Italy,
Ph. Laurence Gouault.

The Fang,
Vail, Colorado,

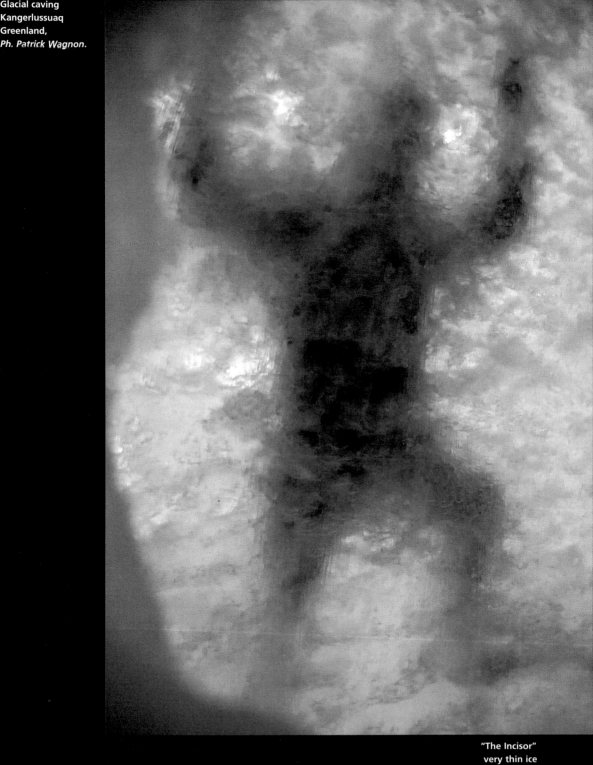

Glacial caving
Kangerlussuaq
Greenland,
Ph. Patrick Wagnon.

"The Incisor"
very thin ice
in the early season
Alberta,
Kananaskis Country,
Canadian Rockies,
Ph. Brad Wrobleski.

"Bubu" Mauro Bole
White Cliffs of Dover
Great Britain,
Ph. Manu Ibarra.

Robert Jasper
White Out, M10,
Lauterbrunnen,
Bernese Oberland
Switzerland,
Ph. Klaus Fengler.

"Fuck the Leashes"
Pitztal, Austria,
Ph. Guillaume Vallot.

Stevie Haston
Arne M9
Norway,
Ph. Laurence Gouault.

"Warm up"
Kirov Ice World Cup 2000
Russia,
Ph. Max Berger.

Beat Kammerlander
Security Check, M8+/9-
Urnerboden, Switzerland,
Ph. Peter Mathis.

Alpinism

Alpinismo

Alpinisme

Alpinismus

Alpinismo

A L P I N I S M

The Phantoms
of Aiguille du Midi
Mont Blanc, France,
*Ph. Florence Lelong,
Jean-Louis Laroche.*

Eiger - North face,
Old Style Climbing
Stephan Siegrist
and Samuel Zeller
Switzerland,
Ph. Thomas Ulrich.

West Tatras

Alex Huber
soloing Bellavista, 9- / A4
Lavaredo North Face,
Italy,
Ph. Heinz Zak.

Waiting for
the next avalanche
First ascent, East Face
of Beatrice Tower
Karakorum, Pakistan,
Ph. Jimmy Chin.

Dorje Lhakpa, Langtang
Nepal,
Ph. Pascal Tournaire.

Stefan Siegrist, David Fasel
and Greg Crouch
Cerro Torre,
first winterascent
of West Face,
Patagonia, Argentina,
Ph. Thomas Ulrich.

Peru,
Ph. Marco Spataro.

Moab, Slickrock Country,
Utah, USA
Noah Bigwood
and Steve Gerberding
celebrating sunset,
Ph. Kennan Harvey.

Refuge at
Envers des Aiguilles
Refuge,
Mont Blanc, France,
Ph. Christophe Bersoullé.

Eiger North Face
Spit Verdonesque 8A,
Robert Jasper,
Ph. Robert Bösch.

Hallucination
Everest base-camp,
Nepal,
Ph. Xavier Murillo.

Characters

Personaggi

Personnages

Charakter

Caracter

CHARACTERS

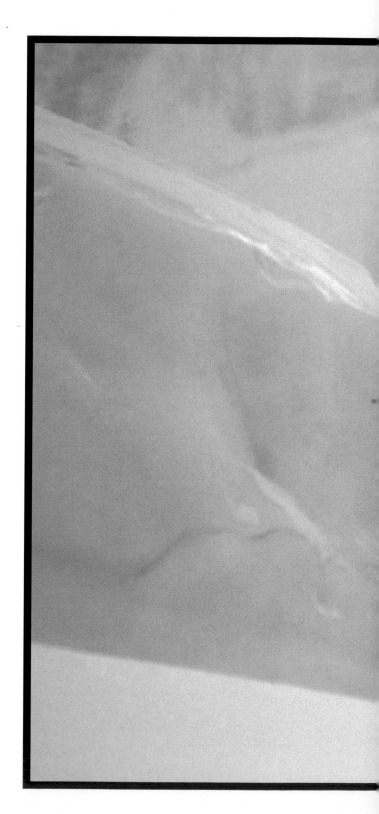

Yeti ?,
Ph. Thomas Ulrich.

"Icelandic horns",
Ph. Mark Buscail -
Rapsodia.

"Icelandic Sauna"
Landmannalaugär
Iceland,
Ph. Sauli Herva.

"Nature calls"
Gressoney
Aosta, Italy,
Ph. Andrea Gallo.

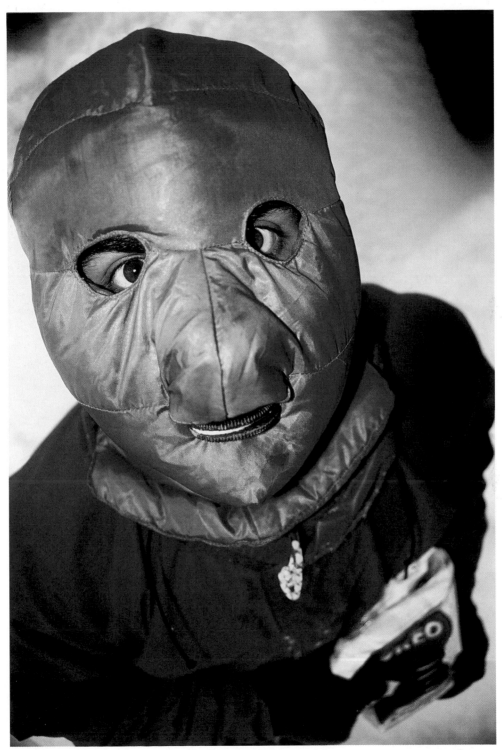

"The Cookie Monster"
Alberta, Canadian
Rockies, Canada,
Ph. Brad Wrobleski.

Farmer, spy or prisoner?
Sausal bei Höch Steiermark,
Austria,
Ph. Manfred Horvath -
Franca Speranza.

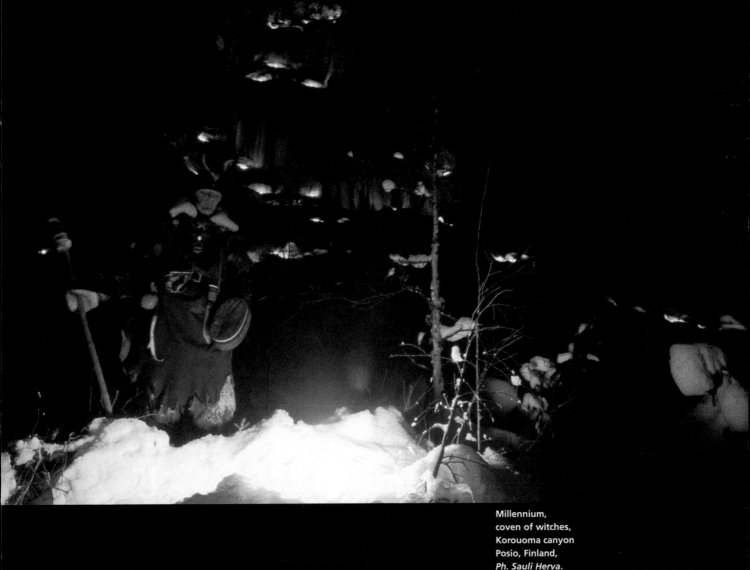

Millennium,
coven of witches,
Korouoma canyon
Posio, Finland,
Ph. Sauli Herva.

**Family portrait,
Kathmandu
Népal,**
Ph. Philippe Rebreyend.

"The Guide"
Pyrenees,

Georg Klocker,
Hohenems-Austria,

Studio photo
Kurt Diemberger,
Cathérine Destivelle,
Silvo Karo
and photographer
Craig Richards,
Ph. Erik Decamp.

Mr. And Mrs.
Bradford Washburn,
Ph. Erik Decamp.

Life

Vita

La Vie

Leben

Vida

LIFE

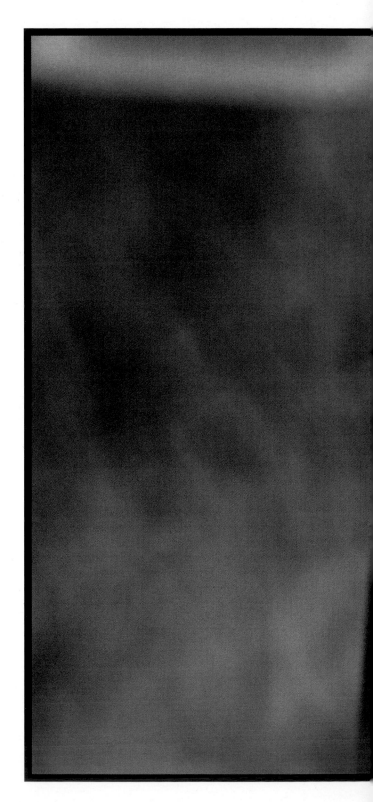

"A coffee break"
Riisitunturi,
Finland,
Ph. Sauli Herva.

Ph. Eduardo Velasco.

Ph. Bruno Sourzac.

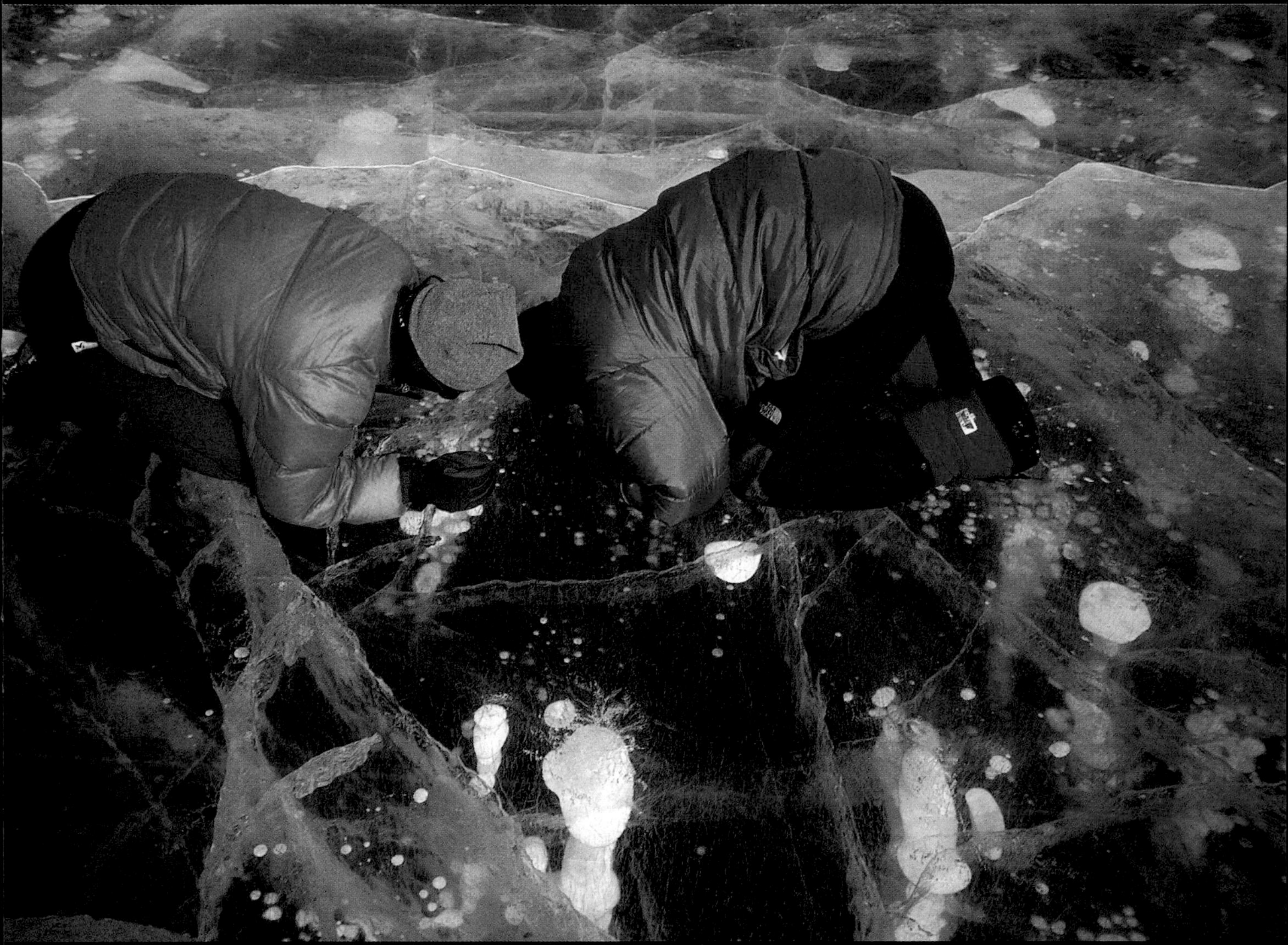

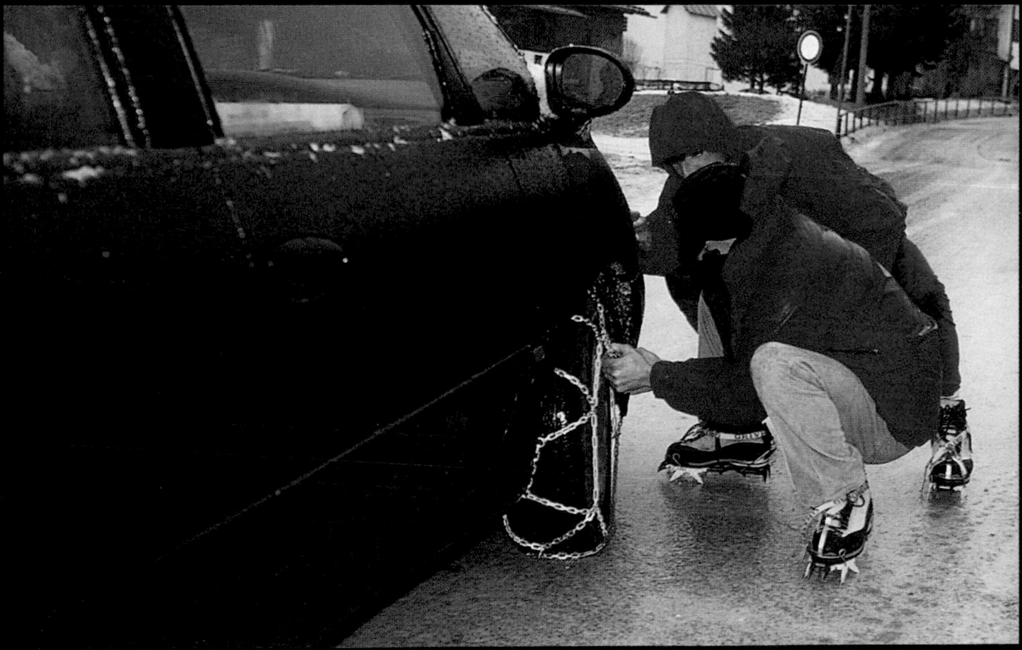

Crampons for four wheels
Pascal Cavoret
and Daniel Du Lac,
Cortina Italy,
Ph. Guillaume Vallot.

"No Smoking"
Old mountain hut,
Ayas Valley,
Italy,
Ph. Marco Spataro.

Mountain hut,
Valsorey,
Switzerland,
*Ph. Laurent Bouvet –
Rapsodia.*

Flower pot!
Uina canyon,
Unterengadin,
Ph. Klaus Fengler.

Flower pot ,
Champoluc, Italy,
Ph. Marco Spataro.

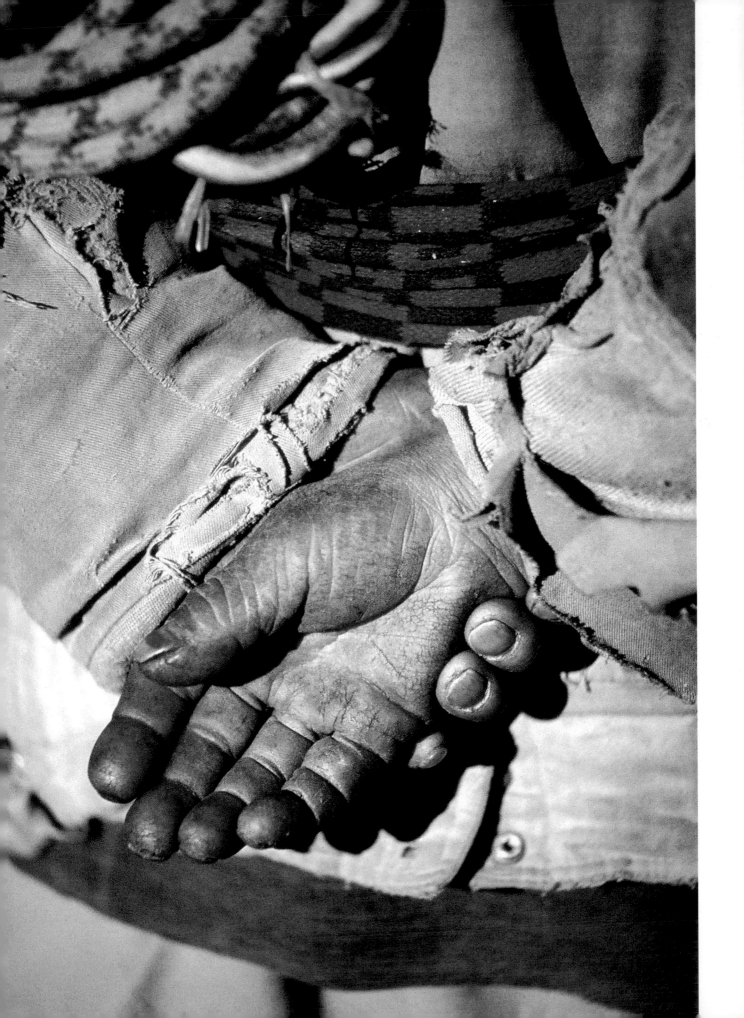

Hard labour
Pakistan,
Ph. Frederik Schlyter.

Hard labour
Austria,
Ph. Heinz Zak.

Chaos

Caos

Chaos

Chaos

Caos

CHAOS

Phone boxes
Ailefroide, Oisans,
France,
Ph. Philippe Rebreyend.

L'Envers des Aiguilles
France,
Ph. Christophe Bersoullé.

Death Bivouac,
Heckmair route
Eiger north face,
Switzerland,
Ph. Robert Bösch.

Nevada   WTO Protest,

"Talon aiguilles",

Daytime
Longyearbyen,
Svalbard, Norway,
Ph. Anders Modig.

Into Russia!
UKK NP,
Finland,
Ph. Sami Savela.

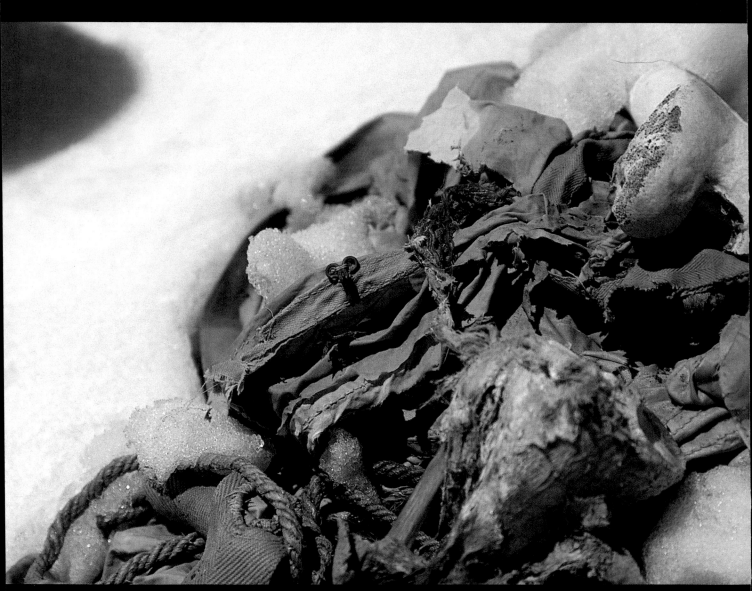
Maurice Wilson

Coal mine n.7
Longyearbyen,
Svalbard, Norway,
Ph. Anders Modig.

Camp IV,
USA,
Ph. Marco Troussier.

Spirit

Spirito

L'Esprit

Esprit

Espíritu

S P I R I T

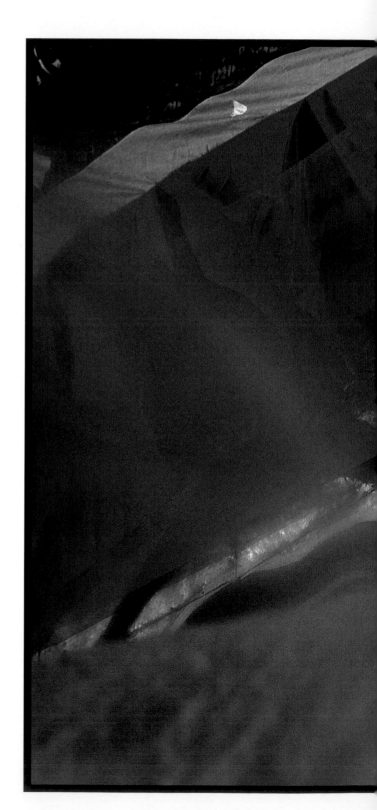

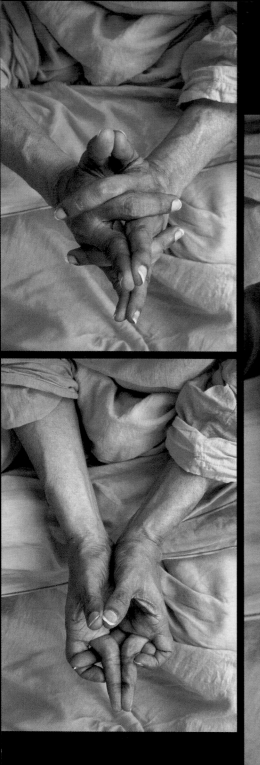

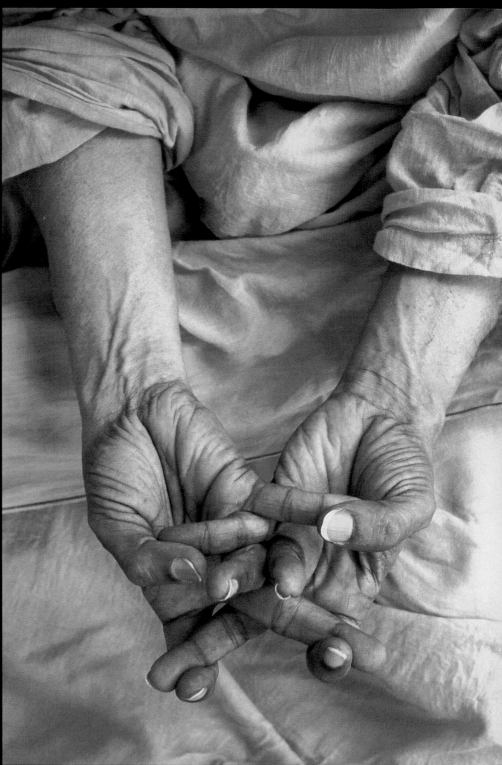

Yoga Mudras
Rishikesh, India,

Snowboard illumination,
Les arcs, Prana,

"Fete du trone",

Virtual Meditation
Labrang monastery, Tibet,
Ph. Catherine Henriette /
ICONE - Franca Speranza.

Winter in Barrow,
Alaska,
*Ph. Galen Rowell -
Franca Speranza.*

Giant's Tomb,
Gallura's Mountain,
Sardinia, Italy,
Ph. Gian Luca Boetti.

Khumba Mela

Sadhus,
India,
Ph. Christian Aslund.

Crow with Rlung-tas
Namche, Nepal,

Lights

Luci

Lumières

Licht

Luces

L I G H T S

Clouds Austria,
Ph. Peter Mathis.

Mt. Tre Pietre
Dolomites, Italy,
Ph. Giandomenico Vincenzi.

Lecco seen from
Mt. Resegone,
Italy,
Ph. Federico Raiser.

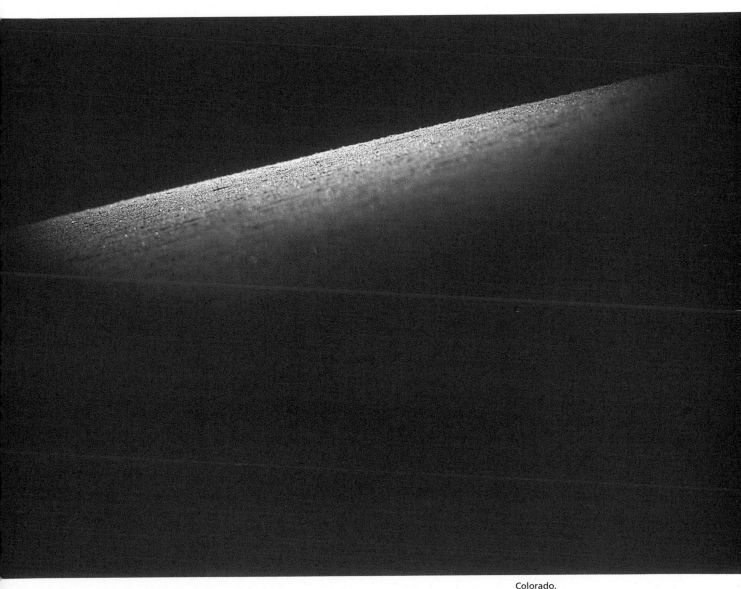

Colorado,
USA,
Ph. Philippe Rebreyend.

Helo Phenomenon
over the ice sheet
Queen Maud Land,
Ph. Anders Modig.

Sunset Everest,
Nepal,
Ph. Sebastien Constant.

Chinook Clouds
Alberta,
Kananaskis Country,
Canada,
Ph. Brad Wrobleski.

Trees with snow
Grenoble, France,
Ph. Philippe Rebreyend.

Puffins,
Bleiskoya, Norway,
Ph. Christian Aslund.

Ama Dablam
Himalaya, Nepal,
Ph. Robert Bösch.

Cerro Torre Reflection,
Argentina,
Ph. Heinz Zak.

Fitz Roy Reflection,
Patagonia,
Ph. Kennan Harvey.

PH. THOMAS ÜLRICH

PHOTO EDITOR
Betta Gobbi

CONCEPT
Gioachino Gobbi

ART DIRECTOR
Eliana Barbera

DESIGNER
Rosa Malfitano

EDITOR
Marco A. Ferrari
Volker Leuchsner
Jean Michel Asselin

PHOTOLITHOGRAPHY
Studio Pro srl, Torino

PRINTED BY
G. Canale & C. spa, Torino

Published by
Vivalda Editori srl

COPYRIGHT
© Vivalda Editori srl, 2000

Yearly Publication
Pubblicazione annuale

P H O T O G R A P H E R S

Andrea Alborno
Loc. Rosselin
11020 Gressan (AO)
Italy
Phone: +39.(0)165.59936
E-mail: albchand@aostanet.com

Christian Aslund
Parkgt. 28
9008 Tromso
Norway
Phone: +47(0)77638231
E-mail:
christianaslund@hotmail.com

Jean Michel Asselin
c/o Glénat Presse
55, Bd. Des Alpes
38240 Meylan
France
Phone: +33(0)476.909707
E-mail:
jeanmi.asselin.verticalroc@glenat.com

Max Berger
c/o Hoehenwerkstatt GmbH -
Eichstr.14
5020 Salzburg
Austria
Phone: +43(0)662.644757
Fax: +43(0)662.64475715
E-mail: info@ice-time.com

**Tullio Bernabei /
Franca Speranza**
V. Melzo, 9
20129 Milano
Italy
Phone: +39(0)2.29402599
Fax: +39(0)2.29406440

Christophe Bersoullé
2, rue Champêtre
31300 Toulouse
France
Phone: +33(0)66013689
E-mail: pimentv@hotmail.com

Robert Bösch
Morgartenstr. 20
6315 Oberägeri
Switzerland
Phone: +41(0)7505755
Fax: +41(0)7500155
E-mail: rboesch@access.ch

Gianluca Boetti
Strada Crosa, 14
10017 Montanaro (TO)
Italy

Phone: +39(0)11.9192172
Fax: +39(0)11.9192172
E-mail: wame@canavese.it

Laurent Bouvet / Rapsodia
1548, Av. Marcel Dassault
74370 Argonay / Annecy
France
Phone: +33(0)450.272165
Fax: +33(0)450.271464
E-mail: rapsodia@mail.dotcom.fr

Mark Buscail / Rapsodia
1548, Av. Marcel Dassault
74370 Argonay / Annecy
France
Phone: +33(0)450.272165
Fax: +33(0)450.271464
E-mail: rapsodia@mail.dotcom.fr

Simon Carter
P.O. Box 49 Blackheath
2785 New South Wales
Australia
Phone: +6.1247877155
Fax: +6.1247877155
E-mail: onsight@flash.com.au

Sylvie Chappaz
15/17 Chemin de la Capuche
38100 Grenoble
France
Phone: +33(0)476.460898
Fax: +33(0)476.460898
E-mail: sylvie.chappaz@wanadoo.fr

Jimmy K. Chin
62 Skyline Dr.
56001 Mankato, Mn U.S.A.
E-mail: jimkchin@hotmail.com

Sébastien Constant
2 rue Pasteur
05100 Briançon
France
Phone: +33.(0)492.203524
E-mail:
sebastien.constant@wanadoo.fr

Erik Decamp
Les Chavaux
74310 Les Houches
France
Phone: +33(0)450.545923
Fax: +33(0)450.545924
E-mail: erik@destivelle.com

Rainer Eder
Scheffelstr. 41
8037 Zürich

Switzerland
Phone: +41(0)1.3625180

Sophie Elbaz / Franca Speranza
V. Melzo, 9
20129 Milano
Italy
Phone: +39(0)2.29402599
Fax: +39(0)2.29406440

Flavio Faganello
V. Serafini, 9
38100 Trento
Italy
Phone: +39(0)461.236676
Fax: +39(0)461.234539

Klaus Fengler
Blissenweg 10a
78476 Allensbach
Germany
Phone: +49(0)7533.997419
Fax: +49(0)7531.86833035
E-mail:
klaus.fengler@kst.siemens.de

Roberto Fioravanti / POF
V. Agnesi, 226
20033 Desio (MI)
Italy
Phone: +39(0)362.306049
E-mail: fi.to@libero.it

Patrick Gabarrou
La Cour Agy
74300 Saint Sigismond
France
Phone: +33(0)450.342485
Fax: +33(0)450.342485

**Andrea Gallo /
Idee Verticali**
V. Maestri del Lavoro, 7
17024 Finale Ligure (SV)
Italy
Phone: +39(0)19.6816102
Fax: +39(0)19.6816507
E-mail: vertical@lnet.it

Laurence Gouault
Chalet Touze - B.P. 32
74310 Les Houches
France
Phone: +33 (0)450545916
E-mail: SLHASTON@aol.com

Eleonora Greco
V.le Lombardia, 96
20131 Milano
Italy

Phone: +39.0338.3834478
E-mail: yoya_1x@tin.it

Kennan Harvey
P.O.Box 882
81302 Durango, CO
U.S.A.
Phone: +1.9703829570
Fax: +19702595559
E-mail:
kennaneharvey@compuserve.com

Andi Hechenberger
Gaisberg 16a
5026 Salzburg
Austria
Phone: +43(0)662.643451

Jakob Helbig
P.D. Lovs Allé 14, 2. Tv
2200 Copenhagen N
Denmark
Phone: +45(0)35.839620

D.C. Henriette / Franca Speranza
V. Melzo, 9
20129 Milano
Italy
Phone: +39(0)2.29402599
Fax: +39(0)2.29406440

**Sauli Herva / Luonnonlaki
Activities**
Kurkelantie 1g
90230 Oulu
Finland
Phone: +358(0)400585317
Fax: +358(0)85571049

**Manfred Horvath / Franca
Speranza**
V. Melzo, 9
20129 Milano
Italy
Phone: +39(0)2.29402599
Fax: +39(0)2.29406440

Manu Ibarra
Strada Larzey - Entreves
11013 Courmayeur (AO)
Italy
Phone: +39(0)165.843714
Fax: +39(0)165.844800
E-mail: manu@grivel.com

Gérard Kosicki
Le Village
38420 Revel
France
Phone: +33(0)476.898447

Eagle Creek TRAVEL GEAR / NATIONAL GEOGRAPHIC SOCIETY

Present the

BANFF MOUNTAIN PHOTOGRAPHY COMPETITION

Over $8,000 in cash and prizes

FOCUS

winners

photo competition

BEST PHOTO ON MOUNTAIN CULTURE, 2000
Horsedrive
Dr. George C. Lo, Vancouver, BC

GRAND PRIZE, 1999
Elk Skull Under Ice
Alec Pytlowany, Banff, AB

BEST PHOTO ON MOUNTAIN ADVENTURE, 2000
Snowboarder Powderdream, Arlberg, Austria
Peter Mathis, Hohenems, Austria

2001

Entries for the 2001 competition must be received in our Banff office by May 31, 2001

VISIT OUR WEBSITE
for more information
www.banffcentre.ab.ca/CMC

Or Contact:
BANFF MOUNTAIN PHOTOGRAPHY COMPETITION
THE BANFF CENTRE FOR MOUNTAIN CULTURE
107 TUNNEL MOUNTAIN DRIVE
BOX 1020, STATION 38
BANFF, ALBERTA, CANADA
T0L 0C0

Fax: +33(0)476.898504
E-mail: g@kosicki.com

**Florence Lelong /
Jean-Louis Laroche**
Saint Jean de Chépy
38210 Tullins
France
Phone: +33(0)47607931
+33(0)476.530545

Tuan Luong / Rapsodia
1548, Av. Marcel Dassault
74370 Argonay / Annecy
France
Phone: +33(0)450.272165
Fax: +33(0)450.271464
E-mail: rapsodia@mail.dotcom.fr

T. Mangelsen / Franca Speranza
V. Melzo, 9
20129 Milano
Italy
Phone: +39(0)2.29402599
Fax: +39(0)2.29406440

Peter Mathis
Erlachstr. 45
6845 Hohenems
Austria
Phone: +43(0)5576.75083
Fax: +43(0)5576750834
E-mail: p.mathis@cable.vol.at

Tim Matsui
4219 Latona Ave NE
98105 Seattle, WA U.S.A.
Phone: +1.2064093069
Fax: +1.2062392042
E-mail: photo@timmatsui.com

Paolo Meitre Libertini
V. Piscina, 5
10040 Volvera (TO)
Italy
Phone: +39(0)11.9857587
Fax: +39(0)11.9853942

Anders Modig
Fredhällsgatan 9
11254 Stockholm
Sweden
Phone: +46(0)8.6739610
Fax: +46(0)8.152057
E-mail: anders.modig@polar.se

**David Munilla /
Freelance**
c/ Arcos 50, 2°C Jerez de la Frontera
11401 Jerez, Càdiz
Spain
Phone: +34(0)956.335172
+34(0)956.870682
E-mail: dmrd@correo.cop.es

Xavier Murillo
Chemin du Truc
38660 Saint Hilaire du Touvet
France
Phone: +33(0)476.086004
Fax: +33(0)476.086004
E-mail: xmurillo@aol.com

Philippe Pellet
Rt du Pt Levis-Enclos du Puits
05330 Saint Chaffrey
France
Phone: +33(0)492240761

Gian Luca Pollini
V. Valdossola, 24
40134 Bologna
Italy
Phone: +39(0)51.434787

Philippe Poulet
La Malossanne - 337, rue du Boutet
38340 Voreppe
France
Phone: +33(0)476.501310
Fax: +33(0)476.500930
E-mail: ppoulet@free.fr

Federico Raiser
V. G. Strambio, 34
20133 Milano
Italy
Phone: +39(0)2.70126509

Philippe Rebreyend
403, Route du Mas
38250 Lans en Vercors
France
Phone: +33(0)476.943291
Fax: +33(0)476.943291

Corey Rich
1608 22nd Street
95816 Sacramento, CA U.S.A.
Phone: +1.916.4470454
Fax: +1.916.4470424
E-mail: coreyphoto@aol.com

Galen Rowell / Franca Speranza
V. Melzo, 9
20129 Milano
Italy
Phone: +39(0)2.29402599
Fax: +39(0)2.29406440

Sami Savela
Kurkelantie 1g
90230 Oulu
Finland
Phone: +358(0)400585317
Fax: +358(0)85571049

Fredrik Schlyter
Rullstensv. 9
Aby; Sweden
61634
Phone: +46(0)11284528
E-mail: fresch@algonet.se /
www.fresch-event.com

Bruno Sourzac
Le Fayet
France

Phone: +33(0)450475765

Marco Spataro
Fraz. Frachey
11020 Champoluc (AO)
Italy
Phone: +39(0)125.308116
E-mail: spatix@tiscalinet.it

**Stéphanie Tétu /
Sylvain Dumain**
81, rue de la Joliette
13002 Marseille
France
Phone: +33(0)4.91914113
E-mail: tetuvue@hotmail.com

Pascal Tournaire
Les Planchons
74700 Cordon
France
Phone: +33(0)1.47112019
Fax: +33(0)450479199
E-mail: PTournaire@aol.com

Treal, Ruiz / Franca Speranza
V. Melzo, 9
20129 Milano
Italy
Phone: +39(0)2.29402599
Fax: +39(0)2.29406440

Pierre-Alain Treyvaud
Rue du Léman, 9
1814 La Tour-de-Peilz
Switzerland
Phone: +41(0)21.9432250

Marco Troussier
8, rue de la Gaieté
13114 Puyloubier
France
Phone: +33(0)442.663796
Fax: +33(0)442663796
E-mail: m.troussier@ffme.fr

**Thomas Ulrich / Adventure
Photography**
P.O.Box 143
3800 Interlaken
Switzerland
Phone: +41(0)33.8234708
Fax: +41(0)33.8232711
E-mail: paragliding@spectraweb.ch

Guillaume Vallot
178, route de Pinet
38410 St. Martin d'Uriage
France
Phone: +33(0)476.597408
Fax: +33(0)476.903708
E-mail: guillaumevallot@lemel.fr

Eduardo Velasco
Los Andes, 8 - 1°C
33213 Gijon, Asturias
Spain
Phone: +34(0)98.5312465
Fax: +34(0)98.5314409

Mario Verin
V. Squadra, 5
23887 Olgiate Molgora (LC)
Italy
Phone: +39(0)39.508125
Fax: +39(0)39.508125
E-mail:
verin.castelli@pop.tiscalinet.it

Giandomenico Vincenzi
V. Zabotti, 4
31056 Roncade (TV)
Italy
Phone: +39(0)422.707535
Fax: +39(0)422.840795

Patrick Wagnon
31, rue Servan
38000 Grenoble
France
Phone: +33(0)476.519012
Fax: +33(0)476.513803
E-mail: Patrick.Wagnon@grenoble.-
cemagref.fr

Vladimìr Weiss
Goetheho 13
16000 Prague 6
Czech Republic
Phone: +42(0)603514579
E-mail: vweiss@atlas.cz

Brad Wrobleski
P.O. Box 100
T0L 2C0 Exshaw, Alberta
Canada
Phone: +1.4036780933
Fax: +1.403.6780933
E-mail: cirque@telusplanet.net

Heinz Zak
Ellmannweg 242
6108Scharnitz
Austria
Phone: +43(0)5213.5128
Fax: +43(0)5213.5128

Wilfried Zwaans / Photodesign
Montrealstraat, 13
7007 BE, Doetinchem
The Netherlands
Phone: +31(0)314.360490

■ Information ■ Tel. ++39 461 98 61 20
■ Tel. ++39 461 23 78 32
■ Internet. www.mountainfilmfestival.trento.it
■ E-mail mail@mountainfilmfestival.trento.it

International Mountain Film Festival The Exploration of Adventure

Since 1952 the Film Festival has used cinema, literature, exhibitions, conferences and open discussion between mountaineers to promote and celebrate the World's mountains, their populations and the rich diversity of their cultures.
The Festival originally founded by CAI and the city of Trento were joined by the city of Bolzano in 1988.
The Festival is an international event with competition open to short, medium and full length films including documentaries and those on specific topics. They are judged by an international jury and compete for the "Genziana d'Oro Gran Premio" dedicated to the city of Trento and for the individual "Genziane" for mountaineering, mountains, explorations and adventure sports. Every year roughly 80 films are shown to the public, including the ones in the competition and those re-showing. The Festival though, is not just cinema, but also includes the publishing of mountain literature. It is a forum that hosts debate between the various protagonists on the international stage of mountaineering and has become an important meeting place representing the intrinsic values of the mountains. Throughout the years the natural environment and the people working within it have been of mainstream importance in the discussions and debates during the festival. The protection of the environment and ensuring its future sustainability are subjects that have been raised time and time again during the festival, not just during the week dedicated to cinema, but also on many other occasions.

■ WE ARE
EXTREMELY GRATEFUL
TO ALL THE
PHOTOGRAPHERS
WHO ACCEPTED
OUR INVITATION
TO COLLABORATE ON
THE MILLENNIUM
PROJECT.

■ SIAMO
ESTREMAMENTE GRATI
A TUTTI
I FOTOGRAFI
CHE HANNO
ACCETTATO
IL NOSTRO INVITO
A COLLABORARE
A MILLENNIUM.

■ NOUS TENONS
À REMERCIER TRÈS
CHALEURESEMENT TOUS
LES PHOTOGRAPHES
QUI ONT
ACCEPTÉ DE
COLLABORER
AU PROJECT
DU MILLENIUM.

■ WIR SIND
ALLEN FOTOGRAFEN
HERZLICHST
DANKBAR, DIE DIE
EINLADUNG
ANGENOMMEN HABEN,
AN UNSEREM PROJEKT
"GALERIE VERTIKAL"
TEILZUNEHMEN.

■ ESTAMOS
MUY AGRADECIDOS
A TODOS
LOS FOTÓGRAFOS
QUE HAN ACEPTADO
NUESTRA INVITACIÓN
EN COLABORAR
CON EL PROYECTO
DE MILLENNIUM.

THANK YOU
FOR YOUR PASSION
AND ENTHUSIASM
THAT YOU HAVE SHOWN
IN GIVING US
YOUR BEST
PHOTOGRAPHS.

GRAZIE
PER LA PASSIONE
E L'ENTUSIASMO CHE
AVETE DIMOSTRATO
FORNENDOCI
LE VOSTRE MIGLIORI
FOTOGRAFIE.

MERCI POUR VOTRE
PASSION ET VOTRE
ENTHOUSIASME À NOUS
CONFIER CE QUE VOUS
AVEZ GRÂCE À VOUS
MEILLEURS
DOCUMENTS.

WIR DANKEN
EUCH FÜR DIE
BEGEISTERUNG, DIE IHR
UNS DURCH ZUSENDEN
EURER BESTEN FOTOS
ZUM AUSDRUCK
GEBRACHT HABT.

GRACIAS
POR LA PASIÓN
Y ENTUSIASMO
QUE HAN DEMOSTRADO
EN DARNOS
SUS MEJORES
FOTOGRAFÍAS.

Printed
in November 2000

Stampato
nel Novembre 2000

Imprimé
en Novembre 2000

Erschienen
im November 2000

Empreso
en Noviembre 2000